THE WAY HOME

DOROTHY H. WELLS

THE WAY HOME

Reflections on life and death

Cover by Sarah Jones

St Paul Publications
Middlegreen, Slough SL3 6BT, United Kingdom
Moyglare Road, Maynooth, Co. Kildare, Ireland

ISBN 085439 413 3

Printed by The Guernsey Press Co. Ltd, Guernsey, C.I.

St Paul Publications is an activity of the priests and brothers of the Society of St Paul who proclaim the Gospel through the media of social communication

Contents

A letter to my unknown friends

Dear Reader

I am deeply persuaded that only when we take death seriously shall we take life seriously, by which I mean that we shall see the things of time in the light of eternity. From this standpoint, people and events take on their right value, some less precious or alarming, some more so.

It can be a great consolation, above all as we get older and realise that our mental or physical powers are diminishing, to recognise that this earthly life is a school, a preparation, a pilgrimage in which we go in God and with God to God, who will be our haven, our home, our eternal delight.

With my loving concern for all of you whom I may meet in these few pages, and a place in my prayers.

Yours in the love of God

The Author

1
On the way

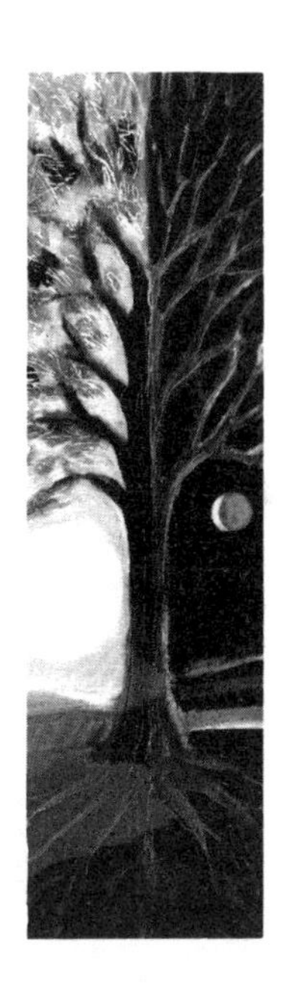

Circumstances

When life is difficult, or monotonous, how easy it is to fall into the thought that differently placed we should be different people, achieving with an effortless and practised touch the creation of the ideal self that we long to become.

At such moments it is a bitter but tonic thought that the circumstances in which we are fretting are the very soil, ordained by our all-knowing and all-loving God, in which at this time we shall grow best. The state of each succeeding hour, whatever it be, is for us the perfect circumstance, if only we will make it so. It is, indeed, the only moment which it is in our power to offer to God, which is what every moment of every human life is for. We cannot endure for his sake now the pain at which we rebelled yesterday, nor yet excuse, with the hope that we shall be patient tomorrow, the angry impatience of today.

The mystery of circumstances is only broken

into succeeding fragments, the mystery of vocation. Each of us is different and each unique, and although we may long for what seems to us a finer and higher way of life than our own, it would not for us, at this instant, be finer or higher, but merely an attempt to be that which we are not – to be, indeed, beside ourselves!

There may of course come to a favoured few among us the vision of a way of God more costly to ourselves, and, as we believe, more in harmony with his will for us. Of such is a religious vocation. But if duty in any form holds us to the path we tread at present, then, whether we can understand it or not, it is good for us to be there.

God has placed us where we are because that is where his plan for the world needs us and the gifts he has given us. He needs what we are, where we are. To distress ourselves over the way we are made or over the part we are called upon to take in life is no compliment to the God who made us.

God's all-embracing love of the human race is calling to each of us in our daily lives. He will see that life is stern enough to temper us, but without crushing us to dust. We need not fear to lose our way in seeking him. We live out our lives under the white radiance of a Benevolence that we cannot see only because we are so little and so blind. Then let us beware lest, in our moments of rebellion, we claim to know better than God does, how it is good for us to live.

The unencumbered heart

Blessed are the poor in spirit,
for theirs is the kingdom of heaven.

Are we wise to be so greedy of permanence and safe possession, we whose very existence on earth demands continual change? Yet from the most trivial of our concerns to the widest and deepest, how often are we not moved by the craving to reach the point where we can lay down our arms and rest? But on earth to be static is to die. Even the rocks are heaved up from the gulfs of the sea, to tower into ranges which in their turn are levelled by the patient snow.

Everything that we possess is lent to us by God. All that we own and are, all that he would have us do and love and suffer, come to us from him. Therefore they must be treasured – but on one condition. We must never lay claim to them as ours, never forget to hold ourselves ready to yield them back into the hands that gave them.

If we try to cling to the gifts of God when he asks for them again, we shall suffer not only the pain of an empty heart but of bruised and bleeding hands. His love is stronger than we are, and for our eternal peace he will not leave us long undisturbed with his good things if we are setting them up to worship in his stead.

Sometimes it seems almost a waste that this earth, which we can never absolutely possess, is so prodigal of beauty. But the earth is not only a pathway; it is a promise. We travel a road strewn with hints of heaven; for beauty, broken and diminished into a million fragments though it be, can yet foreshadow Absolute Beauty. Why must we linger to make our packs heavy with scattered handfuls of treasure when we may run more swiftly unladen to where Beauty awaits us at the journey's end?

It is our duty to reverence the roadways of earth because they lead to God, and to try to make them safer and plainer going, so that those who come after may travel the better because we have gone before. But we may not be possessive even over good works. They must be done in passing, and forgotten, and left behind.

Moreover, we journey through life not as travellers only, but as pilgrims, whose wayfaring is a work of penitence. It is not by sleeping in green gardens that we shall find strength to scale the mountains of God, nor, if we drink too deep on the waters of earth, shall we thirst for the springs of heaven.

It is our sovereign need to learn from pain while pain can teach us, and to keep our hearts empty that they may be filled with God. It is not riches but freedom from enslavement of riches that will set us on our way to heaven; and the staff in our hand must not be contentment but courage.

Money

To know God, if only very dimly, and to love him, if only very faintly, must lead us to the beginnings of trust. And to trust God is the only wise answer to the problem of money.

Do we not all sometimes dream of having enough money to enable us to stop worrying about it? If we do, it will be well to realise that this is one of the dreams that can never come true! The more money we have, the more things we shall want. If we become better off, the wants that did not trouble us because they were so far out of reach suddenly become just within our grasp. So we go on struggling, though now for different objectives, and are no nearer at all to the peace of mind that we had hoped increased prosperity would bring us.

We all seem well off to those who have less than ourselves. They would probably be astonished to know that we have to budget as anxiously as they, in order to pay for our more luxurious ideal of the necessary minimum. So, most probably, do those who seem to us to be really well-to-do. We all demand as much of this world's goods as our money can be stretched to buy. We all worry because there is so small a margin – or no margin at all. We all long for more and fear that we may one day have to try to manage upon less. Our incomes may be very different, but our worries are all very much alike. For man was not made to be satisfied with this world's goods, however obstinately he goes on trying to reach that non-existent point at which he will suddenly find that he has got enough!

The less we demand of the world around us, the more peace we shall have. We can never get enough, but we can try to stop being so greedy. A favourite device of the devil seems to be to whisper in our ear that when we have got just this one thing more we shall be content to stop collecting and able to turn to serving God! Yet we need so little, though we demand so much; and by not getting whatever, on however splendid a scale, shall we achieve freedom from worry.

What do we really need in order to live? The answer is different for every one of us. That we all have certain basic needs to keep us from perishing from exposure or starvation is obvious, but in order to live it is scarcely enough for most of us just not to be dying of hunger or cold! Broadly speaking, what we need for life, over and above what is necessary for mere survival, is that our companions, surroundings, food, pleasures, activities, etc. should not be too widely different from those with which we were brought up. What particular manner and level of life is normal to us does not greatly matter. What does matter is if we find ourselves forced into a way of life in which our natural friends among God's children and creatures are barred from us – either because we can no longer afford them or because we have persuaded ourselves that they are no longer appropriate. We survive bodily, no doubt, but our needs as rational and spiritual creatures are not being adequately met. It is then that we become exiles, and that change of fortune, either for better or for worse, may have to be endured with fortitude because it is real suffering.

For most of us, however, no such dramatic upheaval threatens. Yet we are faced constantly, and sometimes in the wakeful hours of the night almost beaten to our knees, by the battle to keep our standard of living recognisably like the one to which we are accustomed. No only the incidentals but also the very substance of our way of life seem to be slipping from us. How are we to meet these basic needs, or else to learn to be contented without them?

The answer is only believable when we have put it to the test. It is to *demand* absolutely nothing of life except freedom to serve God. Christ told us so two thousand years ago: 'Seek ye first the kingdom of God and his righteousness and all these things shall be added unto you.' But it sounds too good to be true. 'ALL these things'? ALL the things which our heavenly Father knows we are in need of? Surely Christ could not have meant it quite so literally as that! So it is surely only common sense to make sure of a few fundamental treasures without reference to him at all. But it is just this furtive grasping which spoils everything. To learn to swim we must release our hold on the life-belt and entrust ourselves to the water. To learn to live we must release our hold on creatures and entrust ourselves to the love of God. What we cannot do is to have it both ways. We cannot both hold on and learn to swim.

So we quite literally surrender to God our claim on our bank balance, our house, our furniture, our personal treasures and pleasures, our career, our marriage, our health, our children and their future, our friends and what they think of us, and everything else that is ours. We give them all back to God from whom they came, and acknowledge that we have no right to them at all. What follows? Do we suddenly find ourselves, like Job, stripped of everything but our sores? It may be so, in a few rare cases where God sees us as a potential St Francis of Assisi, and if it should come to that we shall have been made to live like that. It is the risk we must take. But most of us are rank-and-file children of God – saints in the making, we hope, but not on the heroic level. So God our Father knows 'that we have need of all these things' which we have offered back to him, and since God is Love it follows axiomatically that what we need (though not, perhaps, all that we think we need) we get. To decree otherwise would be neither merciful nor just, and God is infinitely both!

We surrender to God all we have and all we are – and he gently puts it back into our hands again to use for him. What is the practical result of our gesture? It is *immense*! We no longer worry, or at the very least we worry much less often and to nothing like the same extent. We are set free from the tensions and torments of writing 'must' against things that we cannot honestly afford to pay for. We pray for them instead. If they continue beyond our means, we shall rest assured that we are not meant to have them. If we are meant to have them, the money will come.

This last statement is not the fruit of pious, wishful thinking. Very surprisingly to us faithless and sophisticated men and women, it proves again and again to be the plain and simple truth. Though he may keep us waiting beyond entirely comfortable limits, to strengthen our patience and test our faith, in the end, if what we want is good for us, the Lord will provide. Often he seems almost prodigal, and gives us so much more than we feel we deserve that his generosity fills us with shame. As well as his grace and the gifts of his Spirit he will put us in the way of getting such concrete things as adequate clothes and house room and school fees – and even a car or a video, if he sees that they will bring us closer to himself. If we will only entrust ourselves to him, he will in his turn entrust us with his creatures. Can we think of a single instance in which a man or woman died of want because they had chosen to serve God? (I do not mean martyrs, like the starved and frozen heroes of Sebaste, whose vocation was to die for him, but those he meant to live and work for him on earth.) At the level of mere logic, God could not both intend them to live and allow them to die. In the same way, he cannot both intend us to flourish and allow us to shrivel. So we shall let the love of God determine our standard of living, assured that he will give us everything we need to grow nearer to him in the full perfection of our nature, but nothing that will 'shut up our eyes with fatness' and entice us out of his way.

There is one danger in this surrender of all our affairs to God. Everything we have is a loan from him that he may ask to return at any moment, but – and this is vital – this does not mean that we are not responsible for what has been lent to us while it remains in our hands. It is our ownership, not our stewardship, that we have renounced. What we are is in part the outcome of how we use God's creatures, and it is our part to make the best of whatever he entrusts to our care. To be 'poor in spirit' does not mean to be less careful but less grasping. And putting the kingdom of God first usually, for us who live in the world, seems to entail at least as much work as putting ourselves first, and not infrequently more! The kingdom of God is promised to the violent, not to the half-asleep. But this violence, like a cyclone, will have a still centre, which will be our trust in the love of God. We shall probably find ourselves working harder than ever before, but we shall find the extra strength we need both in the power of God's grace and, perhaps more immediately to be noticed, in the energy which is now set free because we no longer use it to worry with. Not until we stop worrying, largely or altogether, shall we realise how huge a proportion of our available strength of body and mind we wasted in this tormenting pass-time.

'All things work together for good to them that love God.' And on this we may build a life-long peace of heart. All we have and all we are *must* be safe if God has them in his keeping; and if he asks us to suffer the loss of something of them, well, that is good too. ‘Though he slay me, yet will I trust in him.’

God has ordained it, and we lie in the hollow of his hand, and his will for us can never be otherwise than the utterance of Infinite Love.

God the Workman

The other Sunday, when saying the Creed in church, I was suddenly struck by the words about Jesus, 'by whom all things were made.' God is spoken of as the architect, the designer of creation. A few days later I was struck by a much humbler sound, that of hammering, coming from a house which is currently being built across the road. The two ideas fused, and awakened not only thoughts but feelings, both of which I shall now try to share with you.

When searching for understanding, it is always easier to work from the familiar towards the unfamiliar. So I will begin with the young carpenter of Nazareth who, had he lived in our day, could have so easily been the man who was hammering away at the woodwork of the new house.

The following facts about carpentry in the time of Christ come from Daniel-Rops' *Daily Life in Palestine at the Time of Christ* (Weidenfeld & Nicholson, 1962):

> The word 'carpenter', in exactly the sense that we use it today, did not exist in Hebrew; but there were 'cutters' or 'workers of wood', and their part in the village was considerable.
>
> The carpenter was much more than a mere layer of beams. *Naggar* in Aramaic meant both carpenter and joiner and in a general sense 'the builder of houses'.
>
> And to this may be added cabinet-maker, carver, wheelwright and plough- and yoke-maker, as well as woodcutter, to begin at the very beginning. We may picture Jesus walking through a wood with a critical eye, picking his tree, taking his axe and cutting it down.
>
> The workshop of the carpenter, of the *naggar* – a workshop like St Joseph's, for example, at Nazareth – had to be equipped for all the kinds of work that could be ordered. One man would come to have the stilt or the coulter of his plough repaired; another would ask for a pergola to be set up along the side of his house; a woman might come to buy a chest or possibly a bushel to measure her wheat, another a kneading-trough, and still another a support for straw pallets; or a mason would come to order jambs and lintels for doors.

Clearly, then, the carpenter of Palestine was a man of parts; he was uncommonly useful and he was very much esteemed.

Will you come with me into Jesus' workshop? We smell the spicy scent of wood-shavings, see the sun striking the curved surfaces of newly-worked timber. We hear a hammer being used. We watch the strong, clever hands shaping, fitting, fastening. It is hard work and the day is hot. As we come in, Jesus wipes the sweat from his forehead, looks up and smiles, waiting for us to tell him what we want him to do for us. We see a real young man hard at work on a real job. We do not see the Godhead in him, though we may find him powerfully attractive.

Yet the Godhead is there, at one with the manhood in the person of the young carpenter, Jesus. 'And by him all things were made.' What does this mean?

The prophets and psalmists often sang of the wonder of God the creator: 'The heavens are telling the glory of God; and the firmament proclaims his handiwork' (Psalm 19:1).

'When I look at thy heavens, the work of thy fingers, the moon and the stars which thou hast established; what is man that thou art mindful of him, and the son of man that thou dost care for him?' (Psalm 8:3-4).

'He who made the Pleiades and Orion, and turns deep darkness into the morning, and darkens the day into night, who calls for the waters of the sea, and pours them out upon the surface of the earth, the Lord is his name' (Amos 5:8).

These writers are struck by the contrast between the architect of the universe and his beloved little creature, man. We can stop there, in a kind of vague wonder, or, having had revealed to us the existence of the Trinity, we can go deeper. Why *by* him?

Everything that exists, everything that happens, is the effect of four causes: the purpose for which a thing is destined; the way or form in which it comes into being; the urge or drive which makes it come about; and the stuff in which the other causes get to work. The potter must have his clay, the carpenter his timber; salvation can only happen in the soul of man.

We are concerned with the second, or formal, cause. In every fact that science can discover, in the working of every natural law, we can see the mind of God, his knowledge, his Wisdom, his Word; in short, the Second Person of the Trinity, who took our nature as the man, Jesus.

In our day, the frontiers of science are being expanded in two directions: the unthinkably vast, as in astronomy; and the unthinkably small, as in the discoveries of the constituent particles of matter. In between, we have innumerable branches of science – physics, medicine, biology, ecology – the list could take up pages. All this, and far more again than we can imagine, is ever-present to the mind of God. It is not strange that these expanding horizons of knowledge are leading many men of science to the brink of wonder. 'There are more things in heaven and earth than are dreamed of in your philosophy', says Hamlet to Horatio; and for 'philosophy', which means 'love of wisdom', we today could well substitute the word 'science'.

Our minds may begin to stagger at this point, but we needn't worry. The wise author of *The Cloud of Unknowing*, a spiritual writer of the Middle Ages, says: 'God may well be loved, but not thought. By love he may be gotten and holden, but by thought, never.'

In other words, though thought may clear the ground, our way into deeper awareness of God is through love. That is why I find great wonder in fusing my thoughts about the carpenter of Nazareth with those about the architect of creation. Such infinite greatness consents to show itself so simple and so small, so that we may see God, the form or way of our salvation, at work, and may not be dazzled. We may watch the architect of the stars and the snowflakes and all the multitudinous wealth and variety of created things, standing in one small room busy shaping a baby's cradle. Well may St Paul write: 'Who, though he was in the form of God, did not count equality with God a thing to be grasped, but emptied himself, taking the form of a servant, being born in the likeness of men. And being found in human form he humbled himself, and became obedient unto death, even death on a cross' (Phil 2:6-8).

We get many glimpses of the Godhead shining through the manhood. Jesus tells us to consider the lilies of the field. How did they appear to the village workman who, as God, was making their beauty possible? We see Jesus doing extraordinary things with matter. A handful of bread and fish is multiplied to feed thousands. He commands a raging storm to stop – which it does, to the awe, almost the consternation, of his friends in the boat. He is the absolute master. Yet, unless help is called for by some special need or danger, Jesus obeys his own rules. In his human nature he experiences hunger and thirst and exhaustion and pain and death, just as all of us do. St Peter says that he was 'a man like us in all things, save sin'.

The two natures of Jesus (if we keep ourselves simultaneously aware of them) make him so much more a person to turn to – to thank him for all that is good, to trust in for forgiveness, to ask for help, to adore. In Jesus, such tremendous knowledge and power are at one with so much tenderness and understanding. In any kind of distress he can be our sheet-anchor. He can share all our hopes and concerns. He can enter into our grief or joy. He knows us and loves us with a human heart that is aglow with the infinite love of God.

Darkness and light

Christmas 1989 was prefaced by a series of very great disasters. For so many people, in Armenia, in Clapham, in Lockerbie, the light must have seemed to have vanished, blown out by a gale of overwhelming horror. This led me to think of darkness and light – of the possible use and value of darkness in making the light clearer and more precious. (I say 'possible', because one can refuse to hope, bury oneself in the grief and gloom, and so deny the good.) But that is not God's way.

In pagan times, long before God's Good News reached mankind, the winter solstice was celebrated as the moment when the sun began, even though so very slowly, to bring back longer and lighter days. Among the nations of the far north, the Yule feast marked the rebirth of hope at the very moment when the winter's dark was deepest.

God has always talked to men in the cycles of nature, but in a hidden way, by parable and analogy. Then came the Incarnation, the Word of God himself made flesh, no longer speaking in veiled terms, in hints and foreshadowings, but with the majestic assurance of Truth himself. Yet God does not dazzle us. He was the 'darkness' to show us the light.

There is a lovely text in the Book of Wisdom which says: 'For while gentle silence enveloped all things, and night in its swift course was now half gone, thy all-powerful word leaped from heaven, from the royal throne' (Wis 18:14-15).

Against the background of the midnight sky the angels sang to the shepherds. The Wise Men needed the night to show them the star. They *needed* the night. Is there a message here for us when life seems full of darkness?

First, let us think of darkness in itself. What are its virtues? How can it be valuable to us in itself?

Firstly, it is a time of silence. It is not against the uproar of the market-place that we can hear the song of the angels. We need darkness and silence. They can be the heralds of the voice of God.

Secondly, it is in the dark that things begin to grow. Seeds waken underground, and, in our hearts, the darkness can be the seed-bed of trust – trust in life, trust in God. How can we learn to trust when we see our way bright and clear before us, when the going is smooth and everything is easy? Men, like the seeds of plants, need darkness in which to grow. If it were not so, would God, the Light of Light, have allowed darkness to exist? As our well-loved and familiar quotation says: 'Put your hand into the hand of God. That shall be to you better than a light, and safer than a known way.'

Yet there are some forms of darkness which do not seem to promise hope of fulfilment. On the contrary, they seem like the towering clouds of dust which follow a huge volcanic eruption, blotting out the very light of the sun. Our pattern of life is broken, our future full of dread. Is this darkness something in which we can see the hand of God?

I firmly believe that it is, though it is not until the clouds have had time to disperse and the dust to settle that one can begin to see it, much less to dare to speak of it to those hard hit by disaster.

On the social, national and international scale, of course, disasters can, though often indirectly, be bringers of great good. The First World War (1914-18) saw the last use of poison gas and of the secret diplomacy in which suspicion found such fertile ground to flourish. The last war saw a great awakening of generosity between neighbours and classes, and also, I hope and believe, convinced mankind that atomic warfare would be suicidal, a conviction which the disaster at Chernobyl did much to reinforce. The fire at

King's Cross will, we hope, lead to much greater safety in travelling on the London Underground. And of the Armenian earthquake, an article in *The Independent* had this to say:

> The West has responded with great generosity to this dreadful tragedy. But much more impressive than our generosity has been the Soviet Union's willingness, even eagerness, to receive it... Not only has it accepted assistance when offered; it has appealed energetically to the West for help.

What a contrast this makes with the former diplomatic climate of contempt and suspicion! Eastern Europe is accepting solidarity with the rest of mankind!

It looks as though human beings have sometimes to be spanked and shaken into using both care and common sense in the practical matters of life, and also into developing the awareness that we are our brother's keeper, which is the only true foundation for satisfactory living in community. In the Old Testament we are accustomed to reading of God's taking drastic measures to bring the Children of Israel back into line. Is this still going on in our day? Is God allowing dreadful things to happen because obstinate man can learn in no other way?

In his book, *A Walk with a White Bushman*, Laurens van der Post says:

I think that instinctively in my own life, through the experience of my own darkness which seemed to me so horrible, I came to realise that darkness, if properly approached, could be the source of the increase of light for me. I think that this is the great mystery of life – that if evil is seen steadily in relationship with the whole of one's being, then it can lead to an increase of good. Good comes through the challenge.

Let us go forward now from Christmas to Calvary. Crucifixion was an ugly and brutal form of execution. On Calvary it seemed to witness to the ultimate failure, not only of man's dearest hopes and designs, but of the very purposes of God himself. It was the most absolute and uttermost moment of darkness in all human history. Yet this is only to see the darkness from the outside. Its true nature was the price to be paid for the light, the Resurrection, the hope of mankind.

In the passion of Jesus we may discover another and more mysterious value of darkness: it is the price to be paid for the light. Usually we can only see this by looking backwards down our past years and seeing our apparent failures and catastrophes in the light of their ultimate results. Dark and light are both essential parts of the pattern of living, but only if we accept the darkness on account of the light. To insist on unrelieved darkness, to stay in it, wrap oneself in it like a permanent suit of bereavement, let ourselves be enmeshed in a tangle of ineffectual self-pity – this makes darkness a true evil, instead of a possible messenger of God. If darkness is not accepted for the sake of the light, its only fruit will be misery.

There is one way in which to accept darkness can be wonderfully comforting. I am thinking now not of the world's sins and sorrows, but of the darkness in which we find ourselves when we try to capture God within the limits of our little minds. Julian of Norwich most wisely says: 'God may be loved but not thought'.

If we are being tempted to break our minds on the nature of eternal and infinite spirit (something the comprehension of which is utterly beyond our powers) it can come as a great relief to realise and accept that our minds can ultimately grasp nothing of God *as* God. (I am not speaking here of God made Man, God's Word come to tell us what we *can* understand). The poet Henry Vaughan writes:

> There is in God, some say,
> a deep and dazzling darkness.

We can rest in that and find our peace. It can be deeply comforting and strengthening.

This quotation, again from Laurens van der Post's book, seems to sum it all up. He is speaking of the part he believes man is increasingly called to play in sharing the work of redemption:

> Now we know that suffering was the lot of God Incarnate and hence also the lawful lot of his partner, man. It is bearable because it is divinely shared and, in the measure in which man freely shares it, it is transformed into the love which transcends all, and is the light of darkness that leads man, in God, to the final wisdom.

In God's good time

I am writing these thoughts in the firm conviction that God does not cheat. Jesus of Nazareth, God in his humanity, knew and used only what was available to a man in his position, in his own time and place. It is true that on very many occasions the Godhead shines through the humanity, to help and heal and enlighten. But Jesus never called on any knowledge or techniques which were not naturally available to him in his human nature, as a Jew of his own time. His God-knowledge and his God-power he used only to read the hearts of men, to warn them or help them or heal them. But all this was done within the narrow human framework of the kind of life God had chosen to live on our earth.

How unexpected, humanly speaking, was the moment in history when God became man. For God could surely have chosen any of the ages of the world for the Incarnation.

In his humanity, Jesus was so truly a man of his own day and his own race. The way he bases so many of his answers and arguments on texts from Scripture is so typically Jewish. Jesus thought and lived and worked like a Jewish villager born in the early days of the Roman Empire. In his carpenter's shop were only the simplest tools. In his house he had only the minimum of primitive furnishings and chattels, and nothing of what we call comfort. When he travelled he went on foot along the stony, dusty roads of his little country. His very liturgical worship in the village synagogue was that of any God-fearing Jew. God could have become man at any moment in human history; yet he chose this one.

Think of all the intellectual, scientific and technical knowledge which Jesus in his humanity chose not to have. Jesus of Nazareth, God the architect of all creation, had never, as a man, heard of America or Australia. For him as for all his contemporaries, the Mediterranean, as its name implies, was the sea in the middle of the world. Jesus' own little country was all he knew of that world. Did he ever read a book, apart from the Old Testament? The whole body of modern science only came into being many hundreds of years after his day. How his agile mind would have enjoyed discussions with the great Greek philosophers, but he had probably never heard of them. He could write, as Scripture tells us, but even if he had produced volumes of teaching, there were no media to print, distribute or broadcast them. His knowledge of history, apart from that of his own people, must have been sketchy or non-existent. His very lifestyle was narrow and limited in every way. Even St John knew somebody at the high priest's court, but the carpenter of Nazareth could count on no influence with the so-called great men of his time.

Supposing God had chosen our day as the time for the Incarnation? How easily he could have flung the truth broadcast over the whole earth, a divine Billy Graham with every resource of modern technology at his command! Imagine seeing his face on television! Jet planes could have carried him in person to every continent. The breadth of modern university education could have afforded him endless marvellous materials for his parables. Along these lines one's thoughts could go on and on.

Yet Jesus of Nazareth saved his beloved world with only the very minimum of simplest tools. Thirty years in a village workshop. Three years as a wandering preacher. Three hours of agonizing and shameful death. God is indeed unexpected in his ways with man!

So much for what Jesus of Nazareth did *not* have. Nevertheless, one can see, to some extent, why his chosen time and place on earth were so supremely right.

Is it presumptuous to say that God chose the first possible moment in history for the Incarnation? If one could attribute such a motive to Divine Providence, one might almost say that God was in a hurry! He simply couldn't wait to come to our rescue.

As soon as he had forged his Chosen People into a monotheism entirely free from idolatry, he came. As soon as the conquests of Alexander the Great had given the then-known world a universal language, Koiné, or a kind of kitchen-Greek, he came. As soon as the dominion of Rome had imposed order on land and sea, built marvellous roads and cleared the Mediterranean of pirates, so that his apostles could travel with every hope of arriving at their destination, he came. As soon as the Diaspora, the dispersion of the Jews, had established colonies of them with their synagogues in every then-known land, and so caused them to flock to the Holy Land from every country at times of festival, he came. To Palestine, a kind of Middle Eastern Poland, or Belgium, through which people streamed in thousands on their journeys, he came. What passes for pagan religions had largely deteriorated into outward forms, superstitions and mystery cults, so that men of intelligence, such as the Stoics, were seeking alternative reasons for the good life in 'philosophy'. At the same time the huge slave-population toiled and died without any notion or hope of the good life at all. To all these he came to bring hope and enlightenment. The land was ploughed, the seed-bed ready and fertile, so God sent his Son to sow his Word among us.

Can we see any similar evidence of God's providence at work in our own lives or in events of which we have had experience? It might be interesting to search our memories a little and perhaps discover such workings-out of the divine pattern in our own lives. What unexpected and perhaps even unwelcome turns of fate have had a profound influence on the way we live today, things which at the time seemed unlikely to expect and hard to explain? Can we look backwards down the years and see something of the beauty and wisdom of the design?

God's economy

The *Oxford Dictionary* defines 'economy' as the 'administration of concerns and resources of a community' (from the Greek *oikos*, a house, and *nemó*, to manage). The sense in which we often use the word today, implying frugality, is only a secondary meaning.

When considering the great Hebrew prophets, one can be struck by the fact that there seemed to be a pattern of circumstances which was common to them all, and which, on further thought, seemed to be the pattern of God's dealings with many. Thus he chose to speak to his people. This was the pattern of apparent failure. Carrying out God's command to speak seemed, in so many cases, to lead through suffering and darkness to death.

I thought of Moses, standing on his mountain looking his last over the Promised Land in which he would never live. I thought of the first Isaiah, ending his days under a king who, by leading the people back into idolatry, was undoing all the good Isaiah had been able to bring about in the previous reign. I thought of Jeremiah, ruthlessly victimised all his life and ending by being most unwillingly carried off to exile and death in Egypt. There was Ezekiel, who spent most of his life in exile in Babylon and had to mourn over the utter destruction of Jerusalem.

I thought of John the Baptist, dying in prison and never seeing the Kingdom of God established on earth. I thought most of all of Jesus himself and his mother on Calvary. If ever there was, humanly speaking, a picture of utter failure, it was the Son of Man dying as a common criminal on that hillside outside Jerusalem. I thought of many martyrs down the ages – Thomas á Becket, Thomas More, Joan of Arc – the list is endless. I thought of a less well-known man whose faith and courage has for years been an inspiration to me – Bishop Challoner, who, at the end of the eighteenth century saw the Catholic Church in England apparently dwindling away and yet never gave up hope.

What use did God make of all this darkness and agony of body, mind and spirit? It seemed to me that he used it in two ways.

First, he used it to temper like steel the souls of his chosen ones. Even of Christ, the Letter to the Hebrews (5:7-9) dares to say:

> In the days of his flesh, Jesus offered up prayers and supplications, with loud cries and tears, to him who was able to save him from death, and he was heard for his godly fear. Although he was a Son, he learned obedience through what he suffered; and being made perfect (that is, comments *The Jerusalem Bible*, having totally succeeded in his task of being both priest and victim) he became the source of eternal salvation to all who obey him.

So God's economy with suffering bears twofold fruit. The suffering and apparent failure are the source of holiness for the sufferers, and they are also the seed of future fulfilment and triumph.

The one who seems to end in failure attains a peak of holiness which, it seems, can be reached in no other way. Courage, faith, love are stretched to the utmost – and in the background God is standing guard over the eternal welfare and glory of his servant. So from the sufferer's point of view, there is no waste of agony. God uses it all. God never wastes anything that we give him with love. The divine economy is in loving and complete control.

And what of the future that lay beyond the death of his beloved failures? The Children of Israel inherited their Promised Land. The Hebrews returned from exile and rebuilt the City of

God. John the Baptist was indeed the herald of triumph. And on the cross, the Son of God saved mankind. In the mystery of God's eternal 'now', in which all time is ever-present (though this is indeed a mystery beyond our small, finite minds during this life) – in his eternal 'now', the suffering and the triumph are one, as the root in the dark earth is the bearer of flower and fruit.

The suffering and the triumph are two parts of the same whole, the same reality, and with them God blesses the pain of the present and the glory of the future.

And what of us? We are not God's great ones, so in us the pattern is on a much smaller scale. But it is there in our lives if, trying to do the will of God is our paramount intention. Both the immediate and the eventual outcome are in his hands. Nothing offered to God is wasted. The divine economy can use it all, and apparent failure in our efforts on God's behalf *may* be the most precious gift our love can offer him. As Dante said, 'In his will is our peace'.

Read Psalm 21 which begins as the most desolate cry of dereliction the world has ever known – and then leads on to triumph. In this psalm the whole pattern is plain to see.

Children of God

God has sent the Spirit of his Son
into our hearts, the Spirit that cries, 'Abba, Father,'
and it is this that makes you a son.

God has created each one of us to share his own life, something which begins on earth and will be perfected in heaven. To share his life. But here, thinking in simply human terms, we come up against a difficulty. One can't share a kind of life that one hasn't got. We should be killed if we tried to fly off the cliffs like a gull. At the bottom of the sea we should drown. We are not birds or fish. We do not share their nature – what they are.

From birth we are created in God's image because we are not only a body and brain but a spirit with a mind and a will. But an image is only a likeness. It is not the thing itself. At birth we have only our natural human life. A very wonderful thing it is. But it is not enough. To share God's life we must have what is for us a super-nature, a kind of life that is higher than our own, God's kind of life.

We all know that the gift of this supernatural life is given to us at Baptism – whatever form this may take. What is so beautiful and splendid about Baptism is that God's kind of life is given to us with his love – a birthday present in the most glorious sense. God's love is the Holy Spirit, whom we speak of in the Creed as the 'Lord and giver of life'. The Father gives us his kind of life, the Son gives us the form of it and the Holy Spirit brings us to birth as God's children.

When we call God 'Father', that one word says it all, because a parent of any species generates offspring of its own kind. Jesus revealed to us the astounding fact that we may really and truly say 'Father' to God, not just as a pious figure of speech but as something real – we are God's children, one of his family.

The truth gives us a great responsibility. To be born is not enough. Natural or supernatural, the new life must be fed, cleansed, exercised, loved. This sets the pattern for our life as Christians and also gives it a kind of divine common sense.

The exercise of our spirit is prayer, and the love too. As a child discovers its parents by living with them and, as it grows, by doing things with them, so we discover God by living with him, and, as and when his will is made clear to us, by doing things with him. This can be great joy but it can also, as we all know, demand great effort. Yet we are not alone. The grace that is God's life in us (some of us call it 'sanctifying grace' – gives help and strength at each and every moment for that moment. The Holy Spirit does not force it on us but he is always there saying, 'Let met help you'. It is we who sometimes forget that he is there.

This grace, feeding and strengthening God's life in us, can come in so many ways – by reading, thinking, praying (alone or with our fellow Christians), through the sacraments, for those who believe in this way, through the example and the needs of other people. It can be like a golden thread weaving all our life into union with God.

But thinking in pictures can be misleading. St Thomas Aquinas, one of the greatest Christian thinkers, tells us three facts about grace. By it we share God's life formally – that is, in the form or way of our life. He also stresses that it is a real, existing fact in our soul. He also says that we share God's life in an analogous way. I quote:

> 'When the same word is used of things that are not themselves the same, though they have enough in common to justify so calling them, they are said to be analogous.'

Obviously, in sharing God's life we do not become little Gods – but the likeness to him is close enough to make it possible for us to share his life.

The supernatural life is not a separate part of us, as if we had two lives in us going on side by side. God's life in us takes our human nature with it into a higher way of living, and it is the whole person that is lifted up. All of us, all that we are, can live with this light guiding us, this fire glowing in us. Our whole earthly existence can be dedicated to this kind of living, each passing day bringing us nearer to the moment when we shall be free of the pressures and problems of time and see our Father face to face in the whole splendour of his Godhead.

On being needed

One of the deepest satisfactions in life is surely the awareness of being needed, finding oneself a square peg in a square hole, being recognised and welcomed because we are available and competent to be used. It can be in personal contacts, in social activities, in the sharing of knowledge, money, hospitality, time. There are so many ways.

All these forms of meeting our neighbour's need demand energy, and many of them call for physical mobility and an alert mind. (All of them also demand a concerned and loving heart, but that is outside the scope of this book, because love is independent of all our other qualities and can outlast them all.)

Jesus warns his followers that they need to take up their cross daily. A cross which is almost bound to come to us as we get older is that of being needed less and less. Humanly speaking, old age gradually changes us from an asset to a liability. From being a support to our family and friends, we may turn into a concern, a worry, a complication in their often busy lives. It is useful to face this fact in advance, because in due course many of us may wake up to the realisation that we need all kinds of help and support to go on living in a reasonable condition. We are no longer a plus but a minus!

Jesus also told us, however, that it is more blessed to give than to receive. Certainly the act of giving generously can be very nourishing to our self-esteem! On the other hand, the act of receiving generously is very nourishing for our humility!

A small child automatically accepts being dependent on others. With many of us, there is nothing automatic about such acceptance. It comes as the fruit of continual conscious and, one hopes, loving effort, made over and over again. But this second childhood does not demand senile decay. On the contrary, it can bring a mature tranquillity which can at times, God willing, help others.

I was reading somewhere recently a commentary on St Paul's words; 'I make up in my own body those things which are wanting to the sufferings of Christ.' The writer pointed out that Jesus died at thirty-three in the full vigour of his young manhood. He never knew old age, with all its physical and mental complications. He never knew sickness, the cares of rearing a family, or the battering of noise and stress, as we know it in our often hectic world. We can offer up pains and disadvantages of this kind, as life faces us with them, to round out and complete the cross-bearing which brings redemption to the Mystical Body of Christ – which is another way of saying 'all of us'. We each have our own small vocation to the Cross, a vocation which nobody but each one of us, as individuals, can fulfil.

This seems to me to make clear a most comforting thought. There has never been a moment in any of our lives when we were not needed – needed not by our fellow men but by God. As each of us is unique, this offering to God of his or her troubles, however trivial, is something no other member of the human race can do for us. There are no substitutes or understudies in the Kingdom of God.

As we find ourselves getting older and, humanly speaking, less effective members of society, it will be prudent to give more and more of our days, and above all of our wakeful nights, to thinking about God, reading about him, talking to him, sharing all that happens to us with him and, best of all, just being with him. In his will is our peace.

It may be that, by his mercy, he will be able to use what feels to us like our emptiness and hopelessness as a channel, through which he can let his Spirit of strength and peace and love flow into those around us. We shall probably know nothing about this. We shall have to live in faith that God does not waste his creatures.

Firm in this faith, we should never allow ourselves to fall into the temptation of thinking that we are superfluous, a nuisance, an encumbrance labelled 'not wanted on voyage'! The evil one may try to stir up our pride, to make us want to feed our self-esteem by trying to live by our own failing powers. But in his will is our peace. To the last breath we draw, we can always, by his grace, be valuable, useful, blessed. We can never stop being needed – by God.

‘No one comes to the Father but by me’

These words are not alarming if we are Christians, who have had the Truth, the Way, revealed to them as Christ. But what of the countless millions who live by other faiths or have no faith at all, those to whom the awareness of the human spirit plays no part in their view of life? Are all these non-Christians for ever cut off from the Father?

In times past this was thought to be so, but in our day, thank God, we see matters differently. Yet Jesus’ words remain. How many understand them?

Everything created has four causes.* There is the *final cause* (what it was made for, its pur-

* To those familiar with the works of Aristotle, I apologise for going into such detail. But not everybody is acquainted with this view of things.

pose, its end); the *formal cause* (the shape, manner, form of its way of being); the *efficient cause* (the force or drive that gets things done, brings them into being) and the *material cause* (the substance, the stuff, on which the other three causes operate).

To take a concrete example, when a sculptor sets out to make a statue the final cause of his action is the statue, the formal cause is the shape he gives it, the efficient cause is his urge to create it, and the material cause is the stuff he works with, such as marble, clay or wood.

In God, we see union with the Father as our final cause ('Thou hast made us for thyself', as St Augustine says in his *Confessions*); the Son or Word is the formal cause ('through him all things were made', as we say in the Creed); the Holy Spirit, Infinite Love, is the efficient cause (the divine energy that motivates all creation); and the material cause (as far as mankind is concerned, what God works on and works with) is each one of us.

The true destiny of every human being born into the world is union with the Father, in Christ, through the power of the Holy Spirit. *We become capable of such a union insofar as we become like Christ*. This is the crux of the whole matter. The Christ-like soul becomes capable of seeing God.

It seems mercifully true that countless non-Christians are becoming like Jesus, even if they do not know it. They try to live by what they believe to be the truth, or, for non-believers, by compassion and concern for their fellowmen. It is *why* we live and the *way* we live which is the key to our salvation or our failure. What matters is to try to live by such light as we have (however limited or misguided) and even to die for it if necessary, as Jesus died, although not many of us are called to be martyrs to this extreme extent.

What we must not do is to deny or disregard our own vision of the truth. If and when we do this, weak and fallible creatures as we are, we must admit that we have done wrong and repent (like St Peter who denied his Lord and wept bitterly when he realised what he had done). We cannot always live up to our light, but we must not habitually exchange it for darkness, however difficult it may be to remain steadfast.

Our way home to God is to try to grow more and more Christ-like, whether we are aware of him or not. The Christ-life is the form our life must take. It is through growing into his likeness that we become capable of living in union with the Father (imperfectly in this life, wholly and gloriously in the next). So 'no one comes to the Father except by me' does not limit the hope of salvation; on the contrary, it extends it worldwide. In Christ, Whether we know it or not, we are on our way home.

The senses at prayer

Many books nowadays speak of the two ways of using our senses – intellectually (the way of the West) and in simplicity (the way of the East). We need both; but in practice we are wise to exercise more the way which comes less naturally to us.

All day long we are seeing, hearing, feeling, and having moments when we smell and taste. Usually, however, we do these things unconsciously (which is a waste) or critically (which is one-sided, and robs us of the peace and nourishment which our senses can bring us).

One of my wise books tells us to 'look at the leaf like a calf'! It means that when we see the leaf we do not begin thinking about it, (Is it healthy? Is autumn coming? Is it botanically interesting? What pigments would we mix to put that shade of green on paper?) but instead we just look at it, let it speak to us of greenness, of light and shadow, of the joy of planthood. We do not analyse but, like children, we accept and receive. We become deeply aware of 'leaf' and let the awareness bring us nourishment and peace. It will. A small spring of joy will well up in us that can easily turn into prayer – wonder, adoration, thanksgiving, praise, love – but always being still in the presence of God as we are still in the presence of his leaf. 'Be still and know…' God can say much to us in the word of a single leaf!

As with our eyes, so with our ears. Moments of utter silence are very rare and very precious. Drink them in and let them carry you to God in the deeps of space or in the centre of your own heart. Usually, however, there is some sound – a clock ticking, leaves rustling, a bird, footsteps, voices, music. Even if our ears are battered with noise – traffic, pop-music – we can accept this and suffer it in love, but non-noise is much better for us and worth seeking out. (Even in London, for instance, a church is usually fairly quiet inside, and this can utter a 'word' of deep peace even for those who do not go there to find God.) Listen to God in every sound. (Incidentally, great music 'prayed' as we listen can sometimes be a tremendous experience, both as art and as prayer.)

Our sense of touch is always with us. Let yourself become aware of your finger-tips, your skin, your muscles and bones, as they sense the chair you are sitting on, feel the rough or smooth, warm or cool, the countless variations of texture and temperature and shape. Eastern people finger 'worry-beads' because they have discovered that their round, cool smoothness is an antidote to mental stress. Teach your hands to love the things they touch, or at least to be aware of them. Enter consciously and peacefully into the pleasure touch can give, and praise God!

We all eat several times a day. As children we are told not to bolt our food, but, as adults, hurry plays havoc with our meals. Food has colour and shape and smell before we eat it – sound, too, quite often; and afterwards there is flavour and texture and warmth or coldness to talk to our mouths. Wake your mouth up! Feel your teeth bite, your tongue taste, your throat swallow, your hungry stomach say 'welcome!' Say grace (which means 'thank you') not just before and after meals but with every mouthful, and your bacon and eggs will feed not only your body but your soul!

Smell? This is, perhaps, the sense we are often least aware of, yet the air around us, as every dog knows, is always full of messages. When you get the chance to smell something good, enjoy it consciously. A wise teacher tells us to buy a small bottle of our favourite perfume and carry round with us a handkerchief scented with it. In moments of weariness or frustration, take it out and sniff. Peacefully allow the scent to give you its beauty. Fragrance is another of God's words. Let him use it to comfort us. It does!

But what of all the ways in which our senses can be disgusted? A crushed fieldmouse on the road, a screaming baby, a sticky plate, burnt porridge, the stink of rotting cabbage? These we accept too. They are the senses' prayers of penitence. We have not deserved a perfect world. Use the unpleasantness to tell our loving God that we are sorry for all that is bad or wasted in ourselves, even while we are, perhaps, coping with the source of the nuisance, if such should be our business.

And pain? Pain lovingly accepted can be a broad highway to the heart of God. Naturally it is our duty to take steps to get rid of it, if possible, because a body in good trim makes us fitter for the service of both God and man. But while pain is there, don't waste it. It is a privilege, because in it God is giving us our share in the cross of his beloved Son.

Cultivate this habit of peaceful awareness, and you may well find yourself less strung up and anxious, as so many of us are these days. Stop frowning, clenching your teeth, cringing with your stomach-muscles, holding your shoulders rigid, curling up your toes inside your shoes. Agonise less over the remote or immediate future by accepting the small realities of 'now'. If there is any beauty in them, welcome them with an inner smile that you allow to warm and comfort your whole being.

From trying to live closer to God by staying awake to his world, two good results may follow.

We shall find it easier to resist some of our temptations. If we have the habit of letting God into our sensations we shall not readily want to use them in a way which shuts him out.

Secondly, once we begin to pray in our senses, to be alert to God in his world, he can perhaps take us more easily with him wherever he wants us to go. God speaks to us in many languages, and the more we recognise his Word (through whom all things were made) in the little words of our senses, the more we shall come to love him.

Love God in a rose, and you can have entered on the way of holiness. It will be your own way, which is also Christ's way in you, the way you were born to take into the eternal love of God who made us.

'God-bathing' – a way of prayer

If we hope to die close to God, we must have learned to live close to him. Jesus called the disciples his friends. One of the surest ways of becoming friends with God is to pray.

Much of our praying is done using words, either those of others, as in a church service, or one's own, when praying alone. All this is good. But there is a deeper, simpler, more direct way of prayer, which uses no words at all.

One summer day I was looking at a happy grand-daughter of mine, sunbathing on the beach. Lying on her back, eyes closed, completely relaxed, she was offering her body to the warmth of the sun and at the same time welcoming it onto her golden-brown skin. She was giving and receiving in one single act.

We can pray like that. We do not need words.

We open our whole being to God's love and at the same time love him in return. We hold ourselves in awareness of his presence. One prays as simply as one breathes, held in a long moment of love.

This way of praying is so peacefully simple. But it is a power in us that we have to discover. When we are learning to drive a car, many factors have to be mastered severally: clutch, gear, accelerator, brake and many more. Then, one day, the separate parts fuse and we have acquired a new skill, we can drive.

The comparison is not perfect, however. Once we have learned to drive, we can always rely on being able to do it. In prayer, on the other hand, there are days when our awareness of God's presence keeps fading or sliding away into irrelevant thoughts. This is so for everybody. The practice of prayer is exactly what it says – we shall be practising all our lives. But the very practice itself *is* prayer. In spite of what it may feel like, no time which we try to give to God is ever wasted. (A baby will bring its mother a fistful of flower heads with no stalks. Not very successful as a bouquet, perhaps, but the love of giving and sharing is there, and that is all that matters.)

To pray like this, what do we need to do?

1. *Relax.* Get your body in a position comfortable enough to let it remain peaceful while you pray.
2. *Slow up your breathing.* Prayer is timeless so we leave all urgent feelings behind.
3. *Ask the Holy Spirit to help you.* In Romans 8:26 St Paul says: 'The Spirit comes to the aid of our weakness. When we do not know what prayer to offer, to pray as we ought, the Spirit himself intercedes for us.'
4. *Consciously 'God-bathe',* trying to let ourselves accept and give love in one single act of awareness.

Pray in time with your breathing. Some people like to say a loving word over and over again, which helps to still one's mind and focus one's heart. (This is a very ancient practice found in many religions.) However the peaceful awareness of one's own breathing can keep one in God's presence without any words at all.

If such prayer is new to you, begin with ten minutes, and, if you feel moved to do so, increase the time gradually. Half an hour is a good space of time to aim at if one has the leisure, but for busy people, ten or fifteen minutes may be all that is possible.

Finally, a very earthly detail! Buy an egg-timer, and set it for the number of minutes you mean to pray. Your little mechanical friend will tell you when your prayer-time is over and will save you from the distraction – sometimes the temptation! – of constantly glancing at a clock. (Many people find this useful.)

Prayer needs energy. Not the energy of effort but the simple energy of being. There are actions which increase it and actions which waste it.

Quietness can re-fuel one. So can consciously enjoying something with our senses. So can peaceful handicrafts. Our mind and heart need nourishment as much as do our bodies, and these things nourish our inner powers.

How do we waste the energy of our mind and heart? Here are some ways, from which we all suffer. However, becoming aware that they are enemies of our peace is a powerful defence.

Negative emotions such as worry, envy, hurt pride, are bad things to dwell on. We may well need God's help here, because they can be hard to lay aside.

Letting ourselves become utterly absorbed in what we are doing and measuring ourselves by our success or failure. Only by doing our best and laying the result in God's hands shall we work in peace.

Worrying about what other people think of us. There is an anxious child in most of us who acts hoping to impress or be noticed, or fearing to be criticised or despised. As we come closer to God it will grow easier to leave the measuring of our worth to him alone.

Being needlessly in a hurry. Sometimes, every second counts. But life is not always urgent. Rushing through our day is a bad habit. As W. Davies says, 'What is this life if, full of care, we have no time to stand and stare?'

Day-dreaming. Planning what to do is legitimate and necessary. But how often does the Walter Mitty in us waste energy in imaginary doings and conversations?

By overfeeding ourselves on the media. This is a problem peculiar to our own day. It is a duty to know what is happening in our world, and recreation is not only good but necessary. But need we be greedy and laze about exhausting ourselves with violent or trivial happenings which are at best a waste of time, even if not damaging to our inward peace?

Conclusion. There is no need to be continually monitoring ourselves, to guard against all these ways of wasting energy. By our practice of prayer we shall probably wean ourselves off them. We shall want to live more and more at the deeper levels of ourselves, and come to have a truer sense of values. If we are making serious daily efforts to pray, God will send us his wisdom and his peace. We shall know that, however weak and ineffectual we feel ourselves to be, we are God's friends.

2
Homecoming

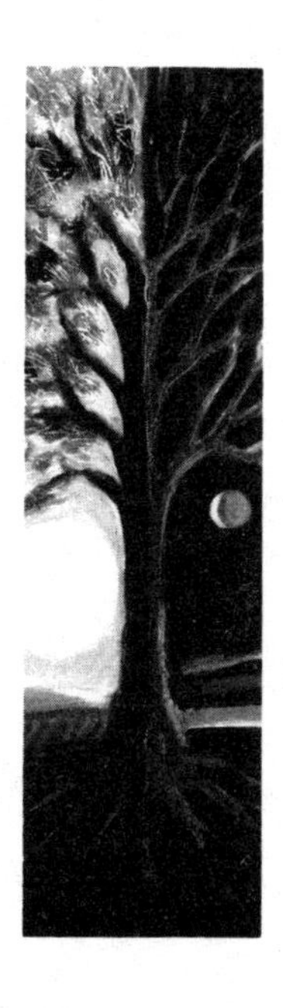

Death on a small island

Some of us really do live on a small island. Not a desert island, however. We can order our eight discs at our local record-shop. The fact remains that many miles of open sea lie all around us. We and our newspapers come here by plane, and our groceries and coal arrive, weather permitting, by boat. We are by nature an independent lot, yet we have to admit that for much of what makes our day-to-day lives possible we are very dependent indeed. Without our lines of communication we should soon be left cold, hungry and isolated.

A few days ago, while weeding in the garden (an occupation which comes hard on the back-muscles but leaves the mind free) the thought came to me that from this point of view people are like islands. We should like to be completely independent and self-sufficient, but we can't be. We have to rely on one another for so many things and, above all, whether we know it or not, we have to rely on God.

We couldn't draw one breath unless he gave us the power to do it. I can't go on breathing except by God's permission. It cuts one down to size!

One day he will stop letting me breathe. There will be nothing I can do about it. I shall have drawn air into my lungs for the last time. My heart, that has been beating so many times a minute all my life, will lie still in my body, just a lump of meat. And my body will begin to go bad. That is a very peculiar thought, hard to believe. But it is happening to somebody, somewhere, every moment of the day.

Where shall I find myself when this happens to me? I don't know anything about 'where', but in some way I shall go on being me. No body, for the time being, anyway. No sight, sound, touch, taste, smell. Nothing perceptible from outside me because death will have shut all these doors to knowledge. Just me – the naked me that is myself, the person whom I have become through my years of living. Just me and God and nothing in between; no eyes to shut and hide what I am thinking. All of me open to God and no escape.

Shall I want to escape? Well, that depends on the kind of 'me' that I am – on the way I lived on this little island of my mortal self before it sank in the sea. I only hope that I shall have learned to trust God enough not to want to run away when I know that he is looking right into me.

I shall certainly feel very much ashamed. How would any of us like another person to see exactly what we think all day long and know exactly why we do things? If anybody had such powers of telepathy he would be the loneliest person on earth. Nobody would dare to go near him!

Of course, God always knows what we are thinking and the strange, mixed-up reasons for most of the things we do. But while we have a good solid body round us we can blanket out the thought of God in a hundred ways. We are very clever at doing this, especially if the idea of him makes us uncomfortable. But when he says 'stop' to my body I shan't be able to do this any more. I shall have nothing to cling to but his love and his mercy. For my own sake, I hope to have practised doing this sufficiently while he still allowed me time.

When the curtain goes up...

Have you ever had to act in a play or perform in a concert? If so, you must have spent many hours rehearsing or practising beforehand. If you stumbled or forgot your lines you had another chance – dozens more chances. That is what rehearsals are for.

However, when the curtain goes up and those rows of empty chairs are now full of people, you have no more chances to practise. Now your performance is real, in full view of the public. The show must go on!

Dying will be like that. Our lives are rehearsals for the moment when the curtain of our body is withdrawn and we are left face to face with God. There will be no more chances to practise, to go back to the beginning and start again. What we have become, we now are, for ever.

Practising the presence of God

I hope to die wanting God, longing for him. I hope that my longing for him will be so strong that the expectation of the moment of total self-awareness in him will outweigh the shock of changing my way of being absolutely. None of us has any experience of being conscious but with no body. It will bring a startling shift of emphasis. It must. But if I have consciously practised asking God to come into my life, into my heart and mind and spirit, I shall, at the moment of dying, be very sure that he is there, and that will be comforting beyond words.

'Comforting' has two meanings in one: soothing and strengthening. God will gentle my passing through death and uphold me as I undergo it, if the habit of turning to him in every emergency is so ingrained that it would never occur to me to do otherwise. Only if this is so may I hope to be sufficiently recollected, except by some very special grace.

The moment of death is, after all, our moment of uttermost weakness. Life as we know it will be disintegrating. So much of what we feel we are will be crumbling away from us. Mercifully, my human spirit is built to survive this experience. It is its nature to go on. How desolate I shall feel if the only powers remaining to me, those of knowing and loving, are weak and uncertain from lack of nourishment and exercise during my days on earth. It will be too late then to do much about it except to cry for mercy, and if such a cry is not the first thing that it occurs to me to do in any crisis, the odds are that I shall be too weak and distracted to utter it.

We need so badly to practise knowing and loving, using the intellect and will which are the powers of our spirit, of our personhood. When everything else has gone, when the 'me' that I am is naked under the loving eyes of God, I hope to be able to fall back on these two powers... to cling to him with my intellect, to say 'yes' with all my will.

To know and love God as he is – this is my destiny. This is what he made me for. This is how I can be eternally and gloriously fulfilled. I hope very much that no days of my life on earth may pass without my having spent some time silent in his presence.

'Be still and know that I am God'... and love me, for I am Love.

Time and eternity

When we are praying, we try to be still... and know. To be still is not always easy in our turbulent times. It may perhaps be a help to realise that the climate of prayer is not in any time at all. The climate of prayer is eternity.

Time is a man's eye-view of existence, for we go from birth to death in what is, for us, a series of consecutive moments. We say that we move out of the past into the present and towards the future. This is a perfectly adequate working concept, and yet there is something very odd about it. We can only do anything in the moment that is 'present' to us – and yet there is no such thing! The past we can measure, and the future too – but what is the duration of 'now'?

There is no 'space' of time, however minuscule, which is neither past nor future but an interval between the two. 'Now' is beyond dimension altogether, having no more real existence in time than the apparent line which marks the horizon of the sea on the sky has in place. Where our view of sea and sky meets, an illusory line seems to divide them. Where our awareness of past and future meets, an illusory interval seems to hold them apart. But 'now' is not a quantity of time. It is a quality of thought.

For practical purposes, we give the name 'present' to stretches of future-flowing-into-past during which some important factor remains constant. 'Now it is Tuesday.' 'Now I am using my typewriter.' 'Now it is 1992.' The unchanging condition, as long as it goes on, makes an illusion for us of an island in the flowing river of time, and from this island we can, in reality, look forward into the future or back into the past. How can we see reality from an imaginary stand-point? Because it is only imaginary when taken as a measurement of time-length. In its true nature 'present' has a much 'deeper' reality than either 'future' or 'past'. Even our dim, earthly perception of 'now' has a faint but unmistakable flavour of eternity.

Animals do not have this awareness of being themselves 'now'. They live submerged in the flow of their own existence. A dog cannot cast its mind back to the lost days of its puppyhood or dread the coming of old age.

It is surely because man has not only a body and a brain like an animal, but also an immortal spirit, that he can have this 'now'-awareness. For the spirit of man can be to some extent free from matter's enslavement to change. It is from the vantage-point of our comparatively timeless soul that we can, as it were, stand outside time and watch it passing.

The continuum, the unchanging thing in my life, is that I am myself. So, whenever I make myself aware of being 'me', I move into my own present. When this awareness becomes heightened into 'me'-in-God, then it is raised from mere self-awareness into recollection. We can easily prove to ourselves that in moments of intense prayer our perception of the things around us can become startlingly vivid, almost as though we had begun to enter into their true reality. (We may not be attentive to this strange fact while we are actually praying, but afterwards we find these small, bright patches in our memory.)

May not this be because in such more or less time-free moments we are aware of things, even if only a little, in the way they are present to the mind of God? Another strange thing is that in our moments of highest awareness of God, it almost feels as though, far from ourselves moving through time, it is time that is flowing through us, flowing through that continuum which is our own, individual, immortal being.

'Now' is how God lives. Eternity is what Boethius called '*tota simul*', that is, 'everything always'. When we pray we can, so to speak, step off the moving staircase of time. It streams past us, now quick, now slow. But we are outside it. We are in the 'now' of God.

In prayer God teaches us how to feel at home in his eternity. It is not too remote from us, because he made us live in him. If we have given ourselves sufficient chances to discover the taste of God's 'now' death will be like a lighted doorway opening to us in welcome, at the end of a long, hard journey. It will simply be the moment when we arrive home at last in the unclouded, eternal presence of God, where, with or without knowing it, we have longed to be throughout all our days in time.

The Way

A human life is a journey, and to travel means to know where we are going. Otherwise we shall be merely wandering, and those who wander with little or no thought of place or direction easily get lost.

Where are we? *In* God, like all created things, though unlike most of them we can be aware of this.

Where are we going? *To* God. Inescapably. But unless we have been travelling towards him intentionally, we may be so shocked when he calls us to a halt in death that dying will hold far more pain and fear for us than trust and joy.

The pain and fear may be total if we have deliberately turned our backs on God in this life; but possibly this is rare. There is evil in most of us; but how far we sin of set purpose is known only to God. Mostly, we pray it is, at any rate, partly a case of 'they know not what they do'.

To leave metaphors, what is this way which we must take if we are to travel safely home to God?

It is loving and caring; using our hearts and minds, practising for heaven with our intellect and our will. If that sounds too abstract, it simply means being interested enough in God to think about him, read about him, talk to him, to accept and use our life as his providence sends it, and to be still and listen to his silence, his presence in ourselves. It also means loving; and he has given us all the world and its people to practise on. We do this for his sake, and also for theirs, because he loves them. They are his people. We do it also for our own sake, because each one of us, single and separately, is infinitely dear to him.

Knowing and loving God can be hard work. Yet there is in every human heart a hunger for the Infinite Eternal, an appetite for God. It may be that much of the restlessness, the sense of frustration, the smouldering anger, that corrode and tarnish so much of human living, are born of this hunger, which is never satisfied because it is never understood.

We who are Christians are much blessed in knowing what is our deepest need. Because we cannot escape from existence without end, horrific or blissful, it is surely only logical, at the very least, to obey God who alone knows all about it, and about us.

'This is eternal life, to know God...'

'Thou shalt love the Lord thy God, and thy neighbour as thyself.'

That is God speaking. And one of his names for himself is 'The Way'.

What kind of peace?

R.I.P. That is what the Church asks for her dead. 'May they rest in peace.' What do we mean by it?

In this life, peace and rest have nearly the same meaning. Struggle and effort have, for the moment, come to an end, and have been followed by tranquillity in which we can recover from our exhaustion and re-create our strength. Weariness, as we know it, is therefore closely linked up with the flesh. We make efforts, become used up and need to recuperate. But is it possible to exhaust one's spirit?

It is surely not in the nature of spirit to get tired. And the mysterious life after our mortal body's death must be more of a spiritual than a physical reality (though for complete human fulfilment both sides of our nature must come into play). So, what do we mean when we pray, 'Eternal rest give unto them, O Lord?'

Because our bodily powers are renewed when we are quiet, we may think of peace as another word for inaction, as if it meant tranquilly doing nothing. But doing nothing, unless we are asleep, seldom stays tranquil for very long. It breeds boredom which in its turn leads to restlessness, the very opposite of peace.

A physical body (in the scientific sense) comes to rest when it has perfect poise, complete equilibrium – when the centrifugal force and the force of gravity do not, so to speak, struggle for mastery, but cancel each other out or combine to give stillness.

Human beings are swayed not by two forces but by countless urges, aims, appetites, temptations, convictions, ideals. We can at times feel almost physically torn by our mental and spiritual wrestlings. But in death, if we have come home to the God we love, all these opposing forces will be stilled and purified and gathered into unison like a choir of many voices singing one perfect music.

Peace, for a human being, is not inaction, but joy in fulfilment. That is the rest of a redeemed soul – not relaxation, which we shall not need, but the enrichment and use of all our powers in a joy deeper than our dearest dreams of bliss. God created us to know and love him. That is what we are for – not for God's sake but for ours. The whole and proper use of all we are, of our entire being, will be a glory of which we can never have enough and of which we can never grow tired.

How does my present way of life sharpen my appetite for the presence of God? The truer and deeper and more constant my longing for him, the more profound will be my entering into peace when I see him face to face.

Blessed are the single-hearted

Men such as tea-tasters, whose trade is to detect and appraise fine flavours, have to avoid smoking and eating or drinking anything that might blunt their sense of taste.

We, whose eternal life hangs on our awareness of God, are wise to avoid anything that will dull our longing for him. It is not that other pleasures are bad in themselves. It is just a question of what we value most.

The practice of the presence of God demands a certain abstinence, a certain denying ourselves other gratifications, a chastity of mind and heart as well as of body. It is as prudent to be careful what we read, listen to, watch on television or allow to dominate our conversations as it is to be temperate over food and drink.

It sounds rather bleak and austere, and indeed that is how it often feels. But feelings easily deceive us. The presence of God, the awareness of him, in the darkness of naked faith alone if necessary, is so great a good that all the pleasure of the world is a grain of dust in comparison.

Yet we are not meant to live without joy – indeed, it is for joy that we are created! So our loving Father sees to it that even in our most arid moments we get a glimpse, sense a touch, become fleetingly aware of a beauty beyond beauty, call it what you will. We know that we are not alone.

Quam dulcis est petentibus –
Sed quid invenientibus!

How gentle he is to those who seek,
But what to those who find!

If the search for God can be sweet enough to make up for all the hardships, what must be the glory of discovery?

God's only child

We are, all of us, God's only children – or, to put it better, each of us is God's only child.

That is not a figure of speech. It is true. Each of us is the only 'me' that he has.

God does not see a football crowd or a concert audience of thousands. He sees a single person countless times over. And on every one of these 'only children' he lavishes the whole of his infinite love and care.

How this can be is far beyond the reach of our imagination or our understanding. But *that* it is so is a fact.

This makes you and me irreplaceably precious to God. My life is the only one he can live in me. My death is the only one of its kind.

This is a challenge. If we ruin or damage the person God has made us, there are no 'spares' to replace us.

It is, I think, comparatively easy to accept that

God loves every person, even when their lovableness is not obvious to ourselves. What can sometimes be more difficult is to feel one's own response to this love. In this connection I was recently much struck by a sentence in Fr Bernard Basset's book, *The Good Life Guide.* He says, 'Had we met Christ, I think we would have been held, not by his looks, his learning or his miracles, but by the ease with which we could be ourselves.'

That is perhaps the deepest and best reason for falling in love – finding another person with whom we feel we need use no defences or disguises; someone with whom we can let go our tensions and relax, someone with whom we dare to be completely open because we are loved *as we are*, simply because we are ourselves.

That is how God loves us. As we get older, weaker, less able to remember and think clearly, more plagued and distracted by the complaints of an ageing body, we may seem less lovable to our fellow men. But not to God.

'He loves me as I am.' That should comfort us very much as our earthly life draws towards its end. Of course we shall have to regret, perhaps agonisingly, that we haven't let the life God gave us make us more like himself. But that cannot change the fact that, at the end of it all, this tired, sick, perhaps confused man or woman who I am is nevertheless always – can never *not* be – the child he is lovingly waiting to welcome home.

The perfect end

'The Lord grant us a quiet night and a perfect end.' Those of us who say Compline (night prayer) ask God for this blessing each nightfall. What are we asking for?

One has a mental picture of the 'perfect end': moving tranquilly from time to eternity, shriven, blessed, prayed for, conscious, at peace with all men, close to those we love. The evening seems a good moment, with the rays of the setting sun glowing in through the window.

But what will really happen?

The answer is God's secret. However, we have one perfect end to think about – that of Jesus on the cross. It was dark, awesome, agonising. But – 'Father, into thy hands I commend my spirit.' This is what makes a perfect end – absolute, trustful, loving confidence in God and, for all but the Sinless One and his Mother, a childlike confidence in God's mercy.

We may not be conscious at the time. What

we can do, however, is to lay our death in God's hands in advance, so that he, who holds all times in his providence, may take us to himself knowing that we too, in unison with our dying Saviour, have said, 'Into thy hands'. So may we go through that strange gateway into the unknown with a spirit at peace and in steadfast, loving hope of the resurrection.

Heaven

Heaven can seem very close to earth in the late spring, especially if there has been a succession of warm, sunlit days tempered by soft little winds. Even in London, light, cool airs seems to come dancing around street corners, breathing out the joy of sun falling across fields where deep hay is whispering and young corn is very green. Even bus-conductors and taxi-drivers, a sombre race, whose moods are the weather-cocks of the city, are benign and friendly, as if the sun had got inside them and was shining out.

In heaven, everybody will be full of delight – not gracious endurance but active, living bliss. We can hardly imagine it, because on earth the sorrowful are always with us.

In heaven, too, life will surely be very simple,

because it will embody the highest truth possible to us. Truth is always simple. It is the hundred wrong answers to our calculations that mislead, confuse and sadden us, but the one right answer brings satisfaction and peace.

In heaven we shall have all the joy that is possible to a risen body and none of the drawbacks of being, in some sense, matter as well as spirit. We shall leave all the machines behind us because we shan't need them.

Our thoughts will take our bodies with them, more swiftly than light travels, if we wish to go – or we can stay and stay in some moment that is dear to us, because our capacity for joy will be fathomless, and however wide and deep the torrent of it that pours into us, we shall always have room for more.

The loveliest truth of all is that we shall share all our joy with Christ. He will delight in the glory of our intellect as we plumb depth upon inexhaustible depth of the beauty of God's reality. His interest, his joy in companionship and mutual awareness will be entirely for each one of us. We shall all have Jesus to ourselves, and yet we shall all be one because our loves will meet in his heart and be gathered into the infinite flame of love who is the Spirit of God.

No doubt the angels are amused when we mortal creatures try to think about heaven. We are like children imagining the wonderful things we shall do when we grow up. Yet there is a huge difference between a child's dreams of a man's life and a man's dream of heaven. The child will not find all that he longed for as the years come towards him. But as heaven enfolds us we shall find so much more than we longed for. It will be the answer to all our dearest dreams, and deep, high and wide beyond them.

There are no earth-words, no earth-thoughts, that are big and true enough to carry the range and scope of life in heaven. And yet it will not be strange to us, because over and above all things will be the joy of being utterly real at last, of living completely true to our whole being with all its needs and powers – of having come home.

'Your death is hidden in my love'

We are always in God's hands. We cannot escape him. If we are too proud to submit to his cherishing we can rebel or we can ignore him. To accept him, as to accept any love, is a little like giving oneself away, in the sense of committing ourselves to another, of having, to some extent at any rate, surrendered our liberty, of having forsworn the right to paddle our own canoe.

By opening our hearts to love we acknowledge that they are empty or, worse, that they are so cluttered with non-love that we must work hard to give love room. Or so we think.

The truth is otherwise. If we let love in, he will make his own place in us. All we have to do is to accept having the clutter thrown out, the dark places lighted and made clean. *All* we have to do? It is the only thing, but it is not an easy thing. There is an evil squirrel in all of us that demands a store against the unknown winter. We dare not accept having God and nothing else.

God and nothing else... But what else *is* there? God is all there is. Why are we so afraid?

'Your death is hidden in my love.' This means not only that final death which closes up the sum of our days on earth, but also the countless little everyday deaths that we undergo in letting God sweep away our hoarded clutter. We lose strength and suppleness of limbs, sight and hearing grow duller, the pleasures of food and drink may bring a penalty of pain, the caring for our treasured possessions becomes a burden. More and more names are crossed out in our address-book, for one cannot write letters to the dead.

Without God, growing old can be desperately lonely. Time is our enemy, a despoiling thief against whom we cannot bar our doors. But say 'God' instead of 'time' and the thief is a thief no longer, because we can only be robbed if what we lose is taken against our will. The treasure we offer voluntarily is a gift.

The cure for the pain of the little daily deaths, as for the great and final death, is to make ourselves into a gift, all that we have and are. 'Into thy hands...' We lay claim to nothing. We have given ourselves away.

But we have not thrown ourselves away.

There is a world of difference between throwing and bestowing. We have given ourselves to Love, and Love cannot help cherishing both the gift and the giver.

From all eternity God has willed me to be myself, so that I might give myself back to him. That is what I am for. That is the flower and fruit of human living, which give it beauty and hold the seeds of deathless life. That is our fulfilment and our peace.

Love is waiting to receive us. From all eternity he has waited. So how shall we be afraid?

'Your death is hidden in my love.'